Kelvin Corcoran

Also by Kelvin Corcoran:

Robin Hood in the Dark Ages
The Red and Yellow Book
Qiryat Sepher
TCL
The Next Wave
Lyric Lyric
Melanie's Book
When Suzy Was
Your Thinking Tracts or Nations
New and Selected Poems
Roger Hilton's Sugar

KELVIN CORCORAN

Backward Turning Sea

Shearsman Books
Exeter

First published in the United Kingdom in 2008 by
Shearsman Books Ltd
58 Velwell Road
Exeter EX4 4LD

www.shearsman.com

ISBN-13 978-1-905700-68-4

Copyright © Kelvin Corcoran, 2008.

The right of Kelvin Corcoran to be identified as the author of this work has been asserted by him in accordance with the Copyrights, Designs and Patents Act of 1988. All rights reserved.

Acknowledgements

'Helen Mania' in this complete version was first published as Poetical Histories 60 in 2004.

'Roger Hilton's Sugar' was published in an earlier version as a chapbook by Leafe Press in 2005.

Some of the poems here have appeared in *Shearsman, Fragmente, Angel Exhaust, New Review of Literature, Green Integer, Onsets, The Gig, Skald, Jacket, Ahadada, Stride, Litter, further evidence of nerves, Quaoar* (with Alan Halsey and Ralph Hawkins) and *Don't Start Me Talking* (Salt Publishing, 2007) – with thanks.

I would like in particular to thank Lynda Black of the Glynn Vivian Gallery Swansea and Ann Jones, the Arts Council Collection, for their help and support in connection with 'Roger Hilton's Sugar' and the *Spotlight on St. Ives* exhibition.

CONTENTS

1 **Helen Mania**   11

2 **The Subsequent World View**
Aphrodite riding on a goat   19
Aphrodite's Bay   20
About My Country   23
From here according to Jenkyns   25
Visitors   26
Alstonefield   29
Basil Bunting and Dylan Thomas in Tehran   34
The Harbour at Night   36
Over the calm, clear shining water   37

3 **Roger Hilton's Sugar**
Setting Out   43
The Language of Art Critics   44
The Hilton Biography – A Selection   45
The Hilton Catalogue – A Selection   46
Radio Hilton   51
Seeing Hilton   52
The St. Ives Section   57
From Botallack Out   59
The Unpainted Hiltons   64

4 **Alexiares**
My Journey to Euripides   75
Odes of Alexiares   81
Interview   84
Alexiares in Exile   85
From Alexiares's Separate Notebooks   91

5 **Ulysses in the Car**
Melanie, I'm in the dark car staring   99
From the Holiday Inn Athens   100
Each green field my god the waves of grass   102

Outside rain rains in this room	103
Lyric voices crowd the sea to sing his mind away	104
The Artemision Tunnel is Two Kilometres Long	105
Another day pours down light in waves	106
When the Spartans came over the mountains	107
Nameless on the water, nobody steps ashore	108
The investigation remains live	109
If we walk by Christeas's tower above the harbour	110
After the final mountains	111
Eroding even the walls of Neriton	112
Coda	113
Notes	114

Backward Turning Sea

Helen Mania

Helen Mania

Yannis told us of the alternative escape route,
Helen and Paris making chariot wheel tracks in Thalami
down to the harbour at Pephnos.

Spartans left waiting at Kranai,
mouths open, bored before the myth
– look at those sparks, like stars eh?

They spent their first night here,
fell upon one another, spent
until the sun came over Taygetos.

Helen set foot on board, trumpets sound
over water, sewing in the grain
the ships of all the world in her wake.

*

Helen didn't want the trouble
safe behind those walls
the army of the fertile plain said so.

I looked at Marathonisi, plotted
the chariot tracks crashing down
from Thalami to Pephnos and the sea.

Helen didn't want it to happen,
then love like Paris arrived.

I looked at the serene harbour
isle of fennel, empty blue mirror,
Helen was not there nor in Egypt.

Honey melting the other side of Taygetos that night.

*

We need a name for this war,
economics won't move our heroes;
plunder is nearer to it but
join our trade war won't swing it.

We need to make it personal.
Control of grain ships through the straights
and increased tax revenue? I think not;
if we had a woman abducted for instance.

In the future they'll see through us,
as if we would turn the world upside down
for a Spartan girl who warmed up the house guest?
Menelaus' hot wife gone wrong.

*

I set my foot in the track
greased slot to smashed Ilium,
one way ride to bliss or exile.

Night of stars, night of revelation
silver jackal sniffing around the door,
storm came smoking off Taygetos.

The house became a boat and
the great green flooded her mind
the island, her dream, floated out to Paris.

Snakes and figs littered the yard.

That morning Helen threw aside the carpet of stars,
that morning Helen stepped aboard.

*

I kept my Spartan girl wrapped up,
hidden under a pile of cloaks
for this languid, sexual periplus.

We drew bright lines across the water
phosphor alphabet dissolving clues,
we lipsticked the mouth of hell below Tanaeron.

Even so she could not be dimmed,
she shone so fair like a bowl of light
desire lifted us like the tide.

Up from the inky black a message,
where fish pick the bones clean and
fields of seaweed denote a continent.

We turned the world upside down:
Menelaus – Where are your divisions now? Stop.
– Your squad cars and riches? Stop.

I left of my own freewill and cannot stop. Stop.

She lay in the boat burning, my beacon,
shaped by heaven,
they built temples in her wake.

*

Who would believe it over a girl?
despite our endless back and forth,
Io, Europa, Medea and the sassy east?
Moon-struck lovers is all we need.

We could get the Egyptian priests on our side,
build a temple to the goddess stranger;
variation as a post-something aesthetic,
she was a ghost above the Skaian gates etc.

I have it now: our brother's loss is our cause.
Make sure you don't catch them,
clear all the harbours down to Matepan;
it's Priam's turn for regime change.

*

We fled in the hour of the furnace
Helen a black outline in the blast
dark one, I see only your face.

Swing the pendulum myth
another woman, another man sail eastward
pass Cythera, ploughing the grain.

Aphrodite came swanning out
attendant gods swim in her wake,
their mouths shaping O O in the eddies.

Oh Helen I loved every woman
to have you, Mr Meat Me, the fool
to find you deep in darkness.

*

My lord they have flown;
I have posted guards to the passes
but who can outrun love?
I'll stick the barb into Menelaus.

I think I hear armour clashing by night,
see smart bomb snapshots of Trojan bunkers;
saturation red hits the air in waves,
reconstructed it's just as real.

Draw up the list of ships
and tilt our western powers into the east;
we can lead our little princes
into the divided meadows of Aphrodite.

*

Helen you are not to blame,
your smoky heart faced the east
the colour rising inside you.

She ascends the steps above the gate,
Helen, the cicadas whisper unearthly,
the sky fuses around the shape of a girl.

Politicians made silent as stone,
remember hope, scratch at lust,
the word wanton dry in their mouths.

She steps forward parting the air
into the live broadcast
wrapped around the world.

She steps forward, pictures the boat
parting the waves, the field of men below,
what? the dream of? the plains of Argos?

She wanted to see her brothers
on the island of Pephnos, they stand in the waves,
guarding the safe passage of her escape.

She steps forward, it is Helen
ascending, her shape makes a window
in the air for the breathless sky.

∗

We saw the sun burn the high meadows
the rain drench the white roots
the wind fuck the come hither waves.

We ran up the goat tracks, breathless
between spurge and aconite and mallow.

Helen you have undone the world
I taste your looks, touch your colour
you were always there, my radiant lexicon.

See how our boat dips and rises
to our shared step aboard
noses out of Pephnos over the endless sea.

We lie together in the seabed
just rippling the light with our breath.

The Subsequent World View

Aphrodite, riding on a goat
keeps me here, anchored in song.

Aphrodite's Bay

I walked in the favour of the gods
the children calling from the water
once out of the bay of the Libyan Sea.

You Egyptians from over there
who can work the gold like us?
make trade in gifts, copper and staples?

We are dripping with this blue
we will prosper for ever
the children call in their drowned language.

There's no dignity wading ashore
the stones roll under foot
and you stagger through endless need.

At that moment, face to face,
sea around your feet, sky falling away,
you must choose, abacus or knife.

        *

I was in the market of market town on Saturday
when I found her in daylight – from where?
Across the Caspian, Anatolia, Sumerian dark wave
against the backdrop of Birmingham bargain stall,
over my head in the tide of singing birds.

Looky, look at this, where'd they get that?
How did that get here and what is your name?
I am not from here, my name trans-Pontine,

I step over the silver thread between two worlds,
I walk to you across water and open the door.

Red dust of Asia perfumed my feet,
the golden hordes at my back look around
their horses nickering for fresh water;
I come from the founders of towns and trade,
I rise up from boom and bust harvests.

I led the way from rickety kids to shining surplus,
I focused the mirage of the blueprint town
across the high table-land, made specialists spring,
dreaming a design to catch the whole world;
our turbine ploughing to the western shore.

*

Today the lesson is English grammar.
It is dangerous to swim in Aphrodite's bay.
Repeat.

Why since then everybody wants to die?
It is the third world war already I think,
bit by bit, what is happening, this music.

Everybody so running to die – why?
You see this aria of Tosca, if they did,
maybe it would make them ok.

And it is dangerous to swim in Aphrodite's bay;
the razor shells will cut your feet,
the currents around the rocks are unpredictable.

Though the water is milky and clings to the skin
like a second body that slides and fits around your own,
long after you have returned to shore.

Today English grammar is heroic film;
the black and white harbour before money arrived,
western coiffure on Levantine heads.

At night I watched the ships unload:
the dovecotes, trinkets and sex toys,
the belief in mythology as fact.

And finally, more than we bargained for,
objectivity in Babylon
brought to book on the banks of the Euphrates.

About My Country

At Actium Octavian invented the West,
half-arsed imperator of the risen state
launched naval blockade, trade sanctions;
those terms rolling over us like white breakers.

*

Around Saddam's Kevlar hat
they gather in dark circles,
stuck on a pole, pre-emptive spite
twisting about in the breeze.

William Blake calls in despair and rubbish,
rubbish is not the answer;
to make this song twenty years,
another city at hand, lit up.

Until we have built between the wars
the syllables of the temple
speaking psalms from the sky,
though Mars is raw on all our heads.

*

I remember when my father was ill with an abscess on his lunges. Neighbours brought food to us; shepherd's pie wrapped in the dish, warm in my hands, and another time ice cream. How can this be? The neighbours standing at the door urging my mother to take the food for her children. Her own stories of childhood sounded like Thomas Hardy. Talking with her brothers, the same faces laughing at the intimate memory of common poverty beaten. And of course there is a limit to what

can be hammered out on the anvil of autobiography – but not the
memory of common poverty beaten.

        ★

They have dug up the bones of Opicinus,
he has photographed the sky above Mogadishu
ambition resting its left foot on Jerusalem;
he is their map maker, surveyor of the oily waters
so that they can ride the Vulva Oceanis.

Those white breakers falling on us, to make the world invisible.
You have been duped by Wahhabi cowboys and Yanky Rapturists.
You were not even a pause in the plan drawn up before election.
You must think of the good to others abandoned by such vanity.
You must think of the schools, hospitals and homes of a better
                                                      nation.

        ★

We knew before Alexander told us
we would arrive in the valley of song,
through familiar villages and secret passes
to find our doubles living like we live.

Inscribed in the mountain air above us
we came to see they were the real people,
we their hungry shadows on the wind
in the valley of song of how we could have lived.

From here according to Jenkyns

From here according to Jenkyns
Sappho entered the western lyric;
I can see the coast of Asia minor,
low blue hills, an apron of light.

The water's not wide, though I can't
get o'er dark imperial Anatolia
where my language was made;
aconite, mallow, fennel at the root.

Visitors

Ivor Gurney

Is that Gurney at the door,
stepping in and out of the light, face down
out of the dark from the bowl of hills
and the impossible message of the stars?

From your submerged green county,
your fortresses of Birdlip and Slad;
sweet Ivor listen, hear your music,
long in the making, brief on the air.

Hear the sea about this house,
the winds lost in the mountains summer long;
from here we map the night and
walk in the light to the houses off the road.

Lee Harwood

On the sea of glass Spyridoula sings Thalassa Mavri
in the Cretan night at the end of your road,
we go under that wave in the war of fish and molluscs.

I name this ship The History of Lost People,
she has her champion aboard;
the cudgelled and heterodox for crew.

Imagine a speech without metaphor,
the transparent borders of new nations;
who knows what happens in that far countree?

Talk keeps our aerial republic afloat,
the benign network from Brighton out
Spyridoula singing Thalassa Mavri.

Mr Halsey's Triptych

bright morning shines across
Mr Halsey's triptych and remotely
not everything is driven

the gentle powdered light
on the worked surface of the picture
a garden for the airy medium

silver bright the unframed thought
let me see it close enough to read
for the aire you sing of generous pith

*

Jack came by for the art event
Jack the lad of morning's spy sir
caught the green boy singing

leaping over the language we speak
disunion Jack with a cigar stuck in him
will not see a halsey in the sky

will not see the worked service
of your debt handsomely paid
the padded waistcoat unbuttoned

★

Alan your work has caught my clever girls
– this is what I want to do in art
– this is how I think I think

I'm looking at the waking world
the march of emblems at my door
comes rattling by 3 by 3 by 3

these ikons open a second front
an unknown country we might
with a racing chance inhabit

Alstonefield

Peter

I've been reading Alstonefield, following you through the nocturnal lanes and fields of the place and the sublime literal you sustain, thinking of Doug Oliver's phrase. It's the voice I want to hear in poetry, free of the grandiose and where everything matters. It is exactly the most intimate and the most shared experience, as you've said elsewhere – rambling in the centre of England with utter irrelevance for good.

Here, after days of a perfect Greek Spring, the storm is over us. So I'm reading *Alstonefield* indoors, with the wild flowers electric leaping along the sides of the roads giving me the come on. The warm rain is falling straight down like curtains of light over the sea.

Yesterday we spoke to the woman who has been restoring what was the family home, a house in the middle of the harbour locked up for twenty years or so. Everything was just left after the big argument. Earlier she had shown Melanie inside, everything was untouched, the furniture, photographs and cups. Now something has been resolved and the place is rebuilt. Her daughter is an architect and she has redesigned the interior. The house sits in the centre of the harbour with a window each side of the fireplace looking out across the gulf to Coroni. Sea light flickers on the ceiling. A sort of exile is over and everything matters, every detail is transformed.

I think you would recognise this story, pack it in your pocket as you go out walking in a Ben Nicholson and see the fit of the stone buildings and the dark fields, wondering through the valleys and limits of a personal poetry. What time is the coach load of professors expected? They've come to remove you and the place for further study, derelict barns and pub car parks filed away in Texas, for imposition on the innocent of America. Will they see a geometry of limestone walls and upland fields in the republic of the poem before all the wars chewed holes in everything we want to hold?

★

In that detailed landscape where you trail, a great breathing space opens up for the senses, for the pleasure of the achieved poem in a candid country. Somebody is dancing half the bloody night and walking around the oval meadow – and there is that man who keeps coming back, on his own or with others. He's doing something.

Another story. Last week in Athens we found the twentieth century ceramics museum, it's in what was the Turkish section by the old market place and new metro. There was something there for you. Demetris Mygdalinos came from a village near the Skamander in Asia Minor. He was a seaman or a diver who shipped up in a pottery centre on the Hellespont. He became a potter and in 1922, with his wife Sappho, fled Turkey and lived in Athens as a refugee. His work was discovered among various cheap factory-made playthings. We see unusual vases, winged donkeys, a naked woman and a piper, a white man on a white horse. Mygdalinos had no wheel nor kiln and he used unfired paints. He sold his pieces at religious fairs and he died in 1949/50 poor and unknown. He made a candlestick with four cats arching up to the candle holder, a two headed horse, a blue tugboat and a winged cat with a red mouth and a red tongue hanging out.

This account comes free from recommendation. You want to look at these pieces over and over, hold them and look at them from every angle. You want their shapes in your hands. You'll understand that this story does not recommend poverty or impersonal victimhood at the hands of international captains, but we see the opposite of Mygdalinos's story, it's obvious and everywhere. No. The sky will not help, nor the soil or trees – about as useful as the discarded televisions to the cats raiding the spider bins last night. If not Mygdalinos then a path opens for the cold and dark airs of the earth at every turn. It closes the heart and it would be easier to drill through the bedrock under this house with a straw than make it live again. If you go down there, into the secret flooded tunnels under the houses where the families come and go, filling and emptying their homes, you would see where all the little metaphors sit around, the metaphors of metaphors, domestic and deceitful, singing for the dull poets.

I think you are right. What return there is from the edge of such nations is not from them but the figures of the dark fields rather. This is before some fool hooked up the ladder after ascent and vanished in an abstraction, leaving behind misfit duties and an elsewhere world view. Against which is this poem of yours, dancing in the oval meadow.

*

In the final part of the poem there's no easy way in or out. You slip into the long valley night walking, humming Gurney perhaps, in the good company of the despised. I remember you were waltzing with a mammal in a serious poem and the vocal bushes had their say. Come on out my little hearties, you gods and insects, let's escape the intervening nonsense through the furrows of night and the Manchester sonatas of memory. I got rhythm – and you Engels? You Cambridge?

Yesterday we went for a walk down the Trachilla road, a walking day in April. There were floods of Spring flowers along the road and under the olive trees a camomile lawn. We walked up onto the strip of land that divides the two bays before you reach the village. I've heard it called the Trachilla Cup but I can't see why. There were two abandoned houses at the top of the hill but the path went no further and we couldn't get down to the bay.

In Trachilla the fruit and veg man rolled up in his van announcing himself with a sleepy megaphone. More people than we imagined lived there came out to buy supplies. We walked along the harbour and an old woman sitting out by her house said – Good day my children. How are you? Are you well? Yes. Yes. It's a very beautiful day. We looked over the steep harbour wall at the Ben Nicholson's exhibited there, lining the shallow, transparent water.

Back out of the village we found the track after the houses on the left. There's an open gateway and you can see the beehives out by the olive trees, this is just as the houses run out. We walked through small, exotic meadow varieties of flowers which you buy in England. We found the path to Palatino Bay, the turquoise water, a place to swim later in the year.

*

I'm walking up and down the dark room reading *Alstonefield* and I can't think how to end this letter. The sea night glitters and a Spring wind rises in the olive trees and I am almost not in Europe at all. What am I doing here? Explain yourself. What are you doing here? There are choirs in the trees, perched – people singing, the Ake, the Dorze, the Irish. They sing, the night is full of holes and all the money has flown away. Roza – How's it going my child? Are you well?

I think that is all.

Basil Bunting and Dylan Thomas in Tehran

1

Are the children singing come back
slap-bang in the black sea of sex of gossip
buoyant on the good ship drink?

Here in 1951, springtide rising,
your silhouette postcard arrived.
How's the oily business treating you?

It's not everyday a ghost sends a message,
despite this absorbent card from Isfahan
blotched with shapely terms.

But this morning, with the circus of waking light
and the traffic of my life on the march,
the poetry god sits down to breakfast.

2

Tehran is depressing and half made;
we went by train to Ahwaz and Abadan,
saw four Iranians on a mud bank
in the middle of the river – contented.

The opium did not touch me,
unlike the beetroot vodka and glycerine beer
which had me flying over arboreal Shiraz,
the city of poets, Hafiz and Sa'di.

Caitlin – could we live together here,
in this dusty, sun-fried place?
Your letter made me want to die,
I went off to the hills with the geologists.

As for our technicolour lie,
the muslims and the nationalists
want shot of the Shah,
and how will we make our money then?

3

When Thomas read for the Anglo-Iranian Society
Bunting was not in the audience, he would return
later that year and go about his own dubious business;
apparently the reading left Mrs. Suralyir shivering with delight.

Why do I pursue this coincidence where none exists?
Both men were entangled in the politics of oil for gain;
if our peers were so involved we would enjoy hating them,
how we would revel in such irrelevance.

Bunting was a spy: Thomas a drunk.
In Country Sleep (1952), the dark enfolded hills of song.
The Spoils (1951), the moment of knowing, free of itself.
Voices drawn from a well deeper than history.

In their great flood of the music of water of music
a chorus explodes; sing sing you reckless bastards,
sing your headfull of singing birds
winging it across the drinkless desert.

The Harbour at Night

In Agios Dimitrios the faultline sounds,
the radio plays and the last car I know
the language of birds calling;
Pephnos rises, Malovos of the shadows appears
and the harbour is an amphitheatre of air.

Open to the west, the sea glitters hidden light,
the fishing boat passes where the dioskouroi stand;
it is Helen longing for her brothers, already immortal;
the hunting owls above them live on darkness
dive into the roots of blood contending.

I listened at the edge of the anti-clockwise sea,
staring into the eyes of the serene empire
the outposts are closed, the captains all gone home,
with Taygetos, the barrier, at my back
sending down green terraces in waves.

The maqams of my brother's music
slide and return on the water, sing amanes at the sky,
and if the rocks follow along the shore to the south,
shatter and explode in the mouth of hell below Tanaeron,
then the whole world goes down with them.

Away in the dark Leuktra is awake tonight,
free city of a walking kingdom;
Ino speaks in dreams in a garden above the sea
making a pathway of living things,
so that Pephnos rises and Malovos of the shadows appears.

Over the calm, clear shining water

Over the calm, clear shining water
with smiling face there came to them the longing
for a bench in a ship to scar the sea,
assaulting the divine.

I am a straight black line, black as the cypress,
tending my relations above the harbour;
soon the ground will open up for the last one,
and I will join them in this earthy gallery.

The radio voices, the cicada telecom, sweep over me,
they mean nothing, I am a black line from the sky;
my son went to the new world, the America
– there will always be men with ambition leaving.

What I don't do won't ever be done,
the shadow of the Far Away One falls on us all;
if my son in the west thinks differently
may the earth rest lightly on him.

I listen to the secret conversation of things,
the village chorus and sea-polished stone
in the light of the pomegranate and fig,
if the bones are white then he is free.

★

Behind Yorgos' gate the sea casts white words
filling our mouths, making us say whatever we think;
all summer long we roll and shout and fall,
go down as the body of water takes a deep breath
and the world comes crashing in wave by wave.

Washed up, abandoned on all fours, shining
in the attitudes of delight, despair, of knowing nothing,
we stand with all the creatures the dark earth feeds;
where transparent altars collapse drink cool air,
the submarine foothills and rivers say welcome.

Open your arms, let Pephnos go, those figs, that life at sea;
Helen's black ship is a shadow passing over you,
the sun, a golden hand trailing in the water,
signals come, follow to the further shore;
and in its wake you swoon and spit and fall.

*

When my brothers stood in the upper world
on that rock with their hands raised,
for all my life they looked like statues.

When my brothers stood in the upper world
they promised safe passage and saved the drowned,
there was no stealth in them, just brave boys.

So when my brothers . . . where are they now?
they wanted nothing of me then
nor in this divinity the other side of Cythera.

Between here and Crete the murex fails
in a deep blue vertigo nations collapse,
there's no end of feeling.

They say the earth trembles still
and I dazzle the armies of the plain,
they walk on insurgent fire at noon.

What means they have for mineral wealth,
but one day the molluscs disappear
and the purple to decorate an empire is gone.

When I rise up into your minds I see
a fault runs around the world,
my brothers walked on water in mercy.

*

We go out into the world in the name of the first wave
breaking over the bow as it dips: blessing; baptism; ambition:
against the countries making conspiracy in their islands.

Call for the ships of Kardamyli and the fifty towns,
the earth opening its little red mouth, set back in the mind,
covered by logistics and the secret invasion of the sea.

For one moment there's no sound on the water,
the roads closed, the electricity cut, and between two bodies
light picks its way down the mountain.

We follow the head of a bird, rising and falling eastward,
sail into the heart of rage and fix our hold upon the lands
as far as the circuit of the earth for the bright pathfinder to guide us.

Inland of the shadowed coast, in the kingdom of rivers,
locked in the contracts of the world below the world
sings the geology of great wealth, starry sex and the life of ease.

Those of us who crossed the border; our seed is not.
Those who sailed into fire; our ships and goods are fallen.
Those who turned back; we don't even say the name of the place.

*

At the slow colouration of the world
milky dawn transposes blue
and the acacia is a net of light
thrown to catch the great iconoclast.

The wall of mountain casts off shadow,
on the opposite arms of the harbour
the chapel and Christeas's tower
stand as blown powers benign.

Where he sets his foot
the music of many drums begins,
the sound's in Thalami I think
no more than girls playing.

Leukothia, steady my sight,
let me align the arms of the harbour
and fix the point in mid blue
where all nonsense is washed away.

In that telescopic ellipse
swim all the living things,
our quick lives coming and going
in the unpeopled cities of stone.

It is light, morning light
comes walking through the village,
out of the folds of the mountain
into the folds of the sea.

Roger Hilton's Sugar

Setting Out

I slip down the road under sea light falling
slam into the giant red women,
ripping green split on both sides
through electric spring wet with flame
to St Ives, the secret island, to find the Hilton.

I sailed a painted boat fit for a boy
against the whole white and crashing world
– darling Bo, thank God you were born,
when I was boy there were horses in the field
and I rode in a cart to cart me off in.

My parents alive, I'm holding on, no hands
as I drift off into the anaesthetised sky.
What's the river doing around the boundary?
I can see you both outside our house,
your faces looking up like white words.

On the secret island, in the middle sea,
two figures dance on the Cape of No Hope,
Hilton sets out, feet first, on the bed of last days,
– the fun is over, what else have I got?
Miraculous pictures leap from his hands.

The Language of Art Critics

My discontinuous line is sexual, intimate, savage,
your fantastic anatomy my vehicle;
this is what they say – beast, charming I'm sure,
show the whole world, why don't you?

As is your life, so is your line,
a fragment made abstract and broadcast;
the human sensation we die for;
my nudes and other animals dancing.

My horses, carts, boats and flowers
such earthly bodies in motion overlap,
run into one another the quick sensation
behind the big secret behind all thought.

Bow down you Greeks, you ghosts;
I am on the last run, with no feeling in my feet.

The Hilton Biography — A Selection

I am lying under a bus in St. Just
– who wants this fucking medal?
It's a curse on me for staleness,
I could use this gravel, textured to my face,
fairer far than palace walls.

I am drinking 300 bottles of life p.a.
and to hell with my perambulation to the pub,
where my nerve endings end I don't go,
in the dim light creeping under the beast's gate
these painted glyphs are mocking me.

I am writing a list of things for you to get,
so get them – the good paint (will gouache fade?)
that Italian bread from Soho, the garlic and good broccoli,
and a decent pen, one that fucking writes.
Forgive me, I am a shit. It is all my fault.

I am making these quick pictures
to keep my family when I am not,
a water soluble inheritance,
to clap their little hands in the breeze
when I am launched into nothing.

I am freezing in this sodding plane,
seven hours to Antibes, freezing for some sunshine,
for the little circus and the afternoon sea;
at last at last, they'll wheel me up and down
and I'll see the god come raging from the water.

The Hilton Catalogue — A Selection

Chaise Longue 1964
gouache, charcoal and coloured chalks.
A small naked woman
dives into the blue pool
chaise longue for you to sit upon,
the water is a naked woman
already for you to swim in.

*

Big Girl 1972
pencil and crayon.
From Big Girl Valley
massive curling breasts,
ohh on her little mouth,
secret dark heart
for you to swim in.

*

Sunbather 1974
gouache and pencil.
Antibes? Yellow woman
white breasts
lolling on the sea
of a yacht
her thighs harbour me
Ahoy Captain Rope.

*

Gouache, card, pastel on paper 1974.
She is looking at me
pink and red and blue,
my friend the snake
above her head.
Her nipple is red
by the rail for pots of flowers,
my Eden, my charmer
– open your mouth.

*

Gouache and charcoal on paper 1974.
White naked bird woman
behind the grassy bank
or sea meadow, populated
by small leggy horses
of orange yellow breed:
we are out of our
paddocks now by God.

*

Gouache, charcoal and pastel 1974.
Is the lizard king
in barbwire jungle
and all the birds of
Cornwall sing,
these buds and leaves
grow out of my body
like girls in Spring
we go down into

the fibrous earth
to return above ground.
If you see the King of Botallack
tell him that all the boys
are thinking of him.

*

Gouache and pastel on paper 1974.
All the exploding
flowers of the world
boomed in one mind,
we are shape colour
looky – how can you resist?
Oh my purple girl.

*

Gouache on paper 1973.
Two in the cart no
horse power pulling
little dog jumpy
rides over
the burning bush,
giddy up into
the dark country.

*

Gouache and charcoal on paper 1974.
Away on the racing green boat
my sea snakes below me

the waves lilt a jaunty angle.
I'm away boys out
into the big oblivion
alone with three clouds grey.
I will leave you the song
of the blue spotted snake
as I lean into the yawn
of the mighty sea calling.

*

Gouache and charcoal on paper 1974.
My red girl locked away from me,
the sex mountains her home
rise over our luxury bed,
our green firework forest
fizzing across the sky.
If I could ride the strong aeroplane,
propel me to her through
all the house descending,
my red girl steps forward to me.

*

Gouache and charcoal on paper 1974.
My name lost
underwritten
no code to read
lost down the lane boy.

*

Gouache and ink on paper 1974.
The room a forest
of shining transepts
around the big cock centrepiece.
Shy creatures peep
smooth branches wave
the organic dance.
Snap Snap Mr Cock
supine for sport
in a chamber of the forest.

*

Gouache on paper 1973.
Written across
an angelic field
of lights
– Fuck you
 Where's my
    Suger
Here it is.

Radio Hilton

The radio that told me about the death of Roger Hilton
was a thousand mile frontier closed down
was nothing left worth looking at
was torture gardens and out of town shopping
was a ghost economy tuned to my heart
was an empty seabed
was a hop skip and jump out of my painting hands
was all the animals falling down
was the work of art itself.

The radio that told me
was an instrument of truth
was the rod and the staff
and the walk we took by the river
shall we bathe again in that blue lick
snaking through the valley of pictures
shall we bathe again
in the waterfall of miraculous bodies
in the valley of all the pictures.

Seeing Hilton

1
Nothing can replace the long, steady gaze,
face to face with the picture.

Swindon Art Gallery and Museum.
Well we'll be closed until 6 March,
for reorganisation, and then yes, I think,
our picture by Roger Hilton will be on show.

The Tate.
I went to the wrong branch,
freezing wind off the river.
No picture, just a postcard of Oi Yoi Yoi.

Bath Victoria Gallery.
Answer machine.
One picture. One question.
No answer.

Nothing can replace the long, steady gaze.

2
Through warm rain and dense traffic
down the southern slope, petrol war stalemate
thickens the Friday night call to air,
to arrive at the moment of seeing – mappa mundi.

1953, oil, neo-plastic work
flat colour from Mondrian daddy,
piling up the words my mind in stripes
of blue of white red white.

Tilting off the edge of England
I'm standing here in the gallery,
all proportion thrown overboard
I see you wave the flag of a new country.

It's 1953, one light floods the dark room
and outside the Atlantic dynamo firing.

3
My cover girl, middle name Matisse,
your anonymous face lifting out of nowhere
has me talking to the wall.

And what is the emotion doing outside?
Slow falling, oh the cold drift towards election
in the western world turning.

Where are you from? Passport? How did you get here?
Archetype, it says. Where's that then?
Floating up from The Levant? The Cyclades?

Head held up, left hand touching the sky
in the storm of stupid questions
the fantastic anatomy falls upon me.

A great passivity settles on the world,
beauty is not difficult, it's as easy as a new earth
rising into view your arms and legs harbour me.

4
Holding the day more firm in unbelief
the sky empties itself on the streets and fields;
I won't travel, snow falling on the frigid circuit,
abstract but suggestive of a figure, a giant.

The country shrinks, clamped down on itself
by the dirty rush to flatter the voting servants;
remote, rigid and slick,
the light thickens and could get arrested.

I won't walk in the capital today,
not even for one painting by Roger Hilton;
I won't emerge from underground near Westminster,
the air full of the sound of reason asleep.

Vision gathers under the frozen bridges,
the picture's far from clear, it's February 1954,
the vertical lines and square shapes
must give way to irregular, expressive forms.

I am only thinking of the journey I did not take.
I am only thinking of the nation that was not made.
I am thinking of the genius of Hilton's painting,
like a brand to stick in the eye of the state.

5
To Swindon on the chuffer train,
milky fog lies in the valleys
clearing slowly for Spring to rise.

I am looking for one picture,
the network firing messages around the cart
and the trees wanting to be green.

This is a ticket less journey,
November 1955, oil on canvas, 44x34;
I should have phoned ahead.

A voice from the store – I can't get it.
It's very black and white and big,
you should come back next year.

A tall Ben Nicholson saved me
like a window into elsewhere,
a composition in lit stone

Left my eyes unencumbered,
and the bowls by Lucie Rie
and almost Cretan pots made me thirsty.

But no Hilton, November 1955,
– I am back on very sober things,
austere to the point of extinction.

Sunk without trace in earth,
rough forms surround a yellow door
poised with calligraphic lines.

The network firing for Spring's revolt.

6
I've walked into this box of summer
and I'm here in the Glynn Vivian telling you,
coastal breath breathing in the circuits of the town
all along Wind Street to Botallack.

Two pictures, six paces and ten years apart,
from the organic forms of a new landscape in '64
you sailed off in two jolly brown boats
into your signal colour and fat red, blue, black.

Reinvent figuration, find something to paint about,
let the white thighed giant dream of heaven;
there's a red wheel to sail by and a red handbag
to keep my ambidextrous hands in.

Roger the green fields, I saw you in the river,
the thermal camera dance, body over body over body,
each imperfect fit, a facsimile of layered truth;
you were pouring water on the sorrows of the world.

The St. Ives Section

The flat screen television of the sea is on
this morning, I think the whole town is
launched at a tilt into the water.

The dead and the living unhoused
founder in the fizzing interference
of not knowing the picture, how composed.

With no recollection of the hovering sky
we're all on the seaslide, what remains is
to tidy up the mess with a few strokes.

*

The revised plan for the Hilton dwelling
will enlarge his lordship's domain;
first we must let in all the plants and animals,
invade the transparent menagerie passage.

But the keening boats and birds won't do it,
not even the limby women and snakes
with their cats and secret harbours;
he will have to jump out of his skin.

*

In the gallery of 18 pictures my delight,
on rough white board the black boat
in a black frame sails on a dark sea.

The figure in the water sees the mast like a cross,
shouts inside an ochre circle making an O,
afloat up to his neck, painted and abandoned.

My boat is framed by an arch or cave,
the bleak mouth edged in thin cerise
says everything about departure.

Away on the horizon, bisected by the mast,
it might be land, an island or promontory
low on the water, a peak made red by the sun.

    *

the spiky tree of big fat amber blossoms
leans out into the harbour where two boats make ready

the sun is written over with the ideogram of a lost language
or a black cockerel, chest out, facing the day

leave now in the red boat, leave now in the black boat
on the first morning spread out under the tree of life

    *

We're all on the seaslide to a new figuration,
last light at the window, across the moor awash
the sea, a thought of my left hand, my right hand;
red dog grin, charcoal corpse and woman akimbo
all ready and waiting in the cart together,
last light on the February walls, on nine pictures dancing.

From Botallack Out

1

Where Hilton wakes restored
in the small acrylic fields of
fabulous women and dancing horses;
Celtic meadows, nocturnal and compact,
tip over the edge of the world
to raise a rampart of dreams
out into the Atlantic morning,
a white line under the door
he walks towards grinning.

For the pleasures of boats on the sea,
of returned desire, of animal breathing,
of abstract animate forms entangled
pouring through the windows,
jump up red dog, jump up:
what else have you got to do?
Your master's scraps fly from the table,
run in the blood of the living,
splash over the loving face.

The tone too is arranged by plan,
plains and contours, the simple colours
of the people's of the sea singing,
who will not let me sleep
rocking the sea all night long;
they ooh and ahh my secret acrobatics
as I cartwheel on the canvas of despair;
at different depths the light changes
aqua, marine, ultra and the green gods.

2

Q1
Is the text of your painting perception itself, so that we see the work of the mind only in the act of painting?

A1
I thought when I was dead
I would not have to explain anything;
green branches shoot from my wrists
instruments of truth or nothing.
Horses caper at my back,
the tide of neuritis rises at night
cold and black licking at the gate:
text? text of what? paint?

Q2
Is it the layer of living things, through which other people and things are first given to us?

A2
Layer of living things, that's good,
up to my elbows in that, paint,
bloody neck more like, Christ,
cat milk spilt bastard fridge broken.
My love the radio's on the blink,
will she ever tune to me again?
The signal's not clear, do nothing,
that record with Caruso singing.
I'm shipped up, skin flaking off
float me away in bloody bedroom,

the hidden life made apparent
free as painting the air blue, red,
vitamin B injections useless
first person lost down the lane boy I.

Q3
Are you conscious of the body as the unperceived term in the centre towards which objects turn?

A3
No getting away from it is there,
especially when it rots raw umber,
nor pens that don't work, empty bottles,
Ronseal awash in the whisky ditch at 3.30 a.m.
fucking objects bite back all the time,
garlic, spinach, blue lake acrylic.
I saw the ghost body under the boat
at one with the waves, the fatal current
all my life, that face emerging:
it's all my fault, I am a shit.
The medicine's a vicious circle,
I sailed around the cirkle islands
swapped pretty boy warbling
for Lord of All Things Moist,
ivy wrapped my every limb afloat.
I bear the young tree sprouting
in my craft or sullen barque,
good dog Spot
              got through another night.

Q4
So, in the sense that all thought is thought about something . . .?

A4
Afterthought I am, I found something
to paint about

writing The Night Letters the
for enjoyment, only for
something to do between pictures,
my figures come breaking out

light will break for another
creation and haddock breakfast
from Botallack out, my figures
left on the table for your edification

3

We came in after a swim,
the rain didn't fall and the sky
rose again into depthless blue,
Taygetos refocused and the temperature
climbed the bronze terraces for summer.

Inside I set up my Hilton gallery,
ripped open an A4 cardboard envelope
stuck three colour printer copies on it
and propped it on the chair,
Oi Yoi Yoi, two boats in the harbour

A third, late gouache, half abstraction,
a brown eyed sun top left and
two blue figures dancing by the ochre band;
I think it's jungle music,
I think it's jig-a-jig time.

Sea-light across the square lifts
at the window, the heavy perfume
of white stephanotis butters the air;
each picture is a revelation
surrounded by torn cardboard.

What they say is unbearable,
beauty burning through our veins;
we wrapped it up for years,
the life that isn't life, a proxy framework,
full of holes and useless.

Look: rip open the envelope,
they spill out, splash and shout,
women and gods and boats
go charging around the house,
– Oi Yoi Yoi, there's a fire.

It snakes under the skin,
sways Arcadia and lifts the tide,
sends birds with messages tree to tree
singing all the names of fire
from the back of Hilton's cart.

The Unpainted Hiltons

You see I am surrounded by these things
a medium like breathing under water,
the Royal Bokhara, the pictures on the wall
I wave as I float by with transparent hands.

My wife's sexy dress hanging there
taken off like a season transformed,
and the organic food jumps into my mouth
as your warm arm falls across me.

The light from the floor landscapes your sleep
and those would be cabbage roses descending,
like red kisses on your perfect cunt
around the dim margin he is on his knees.

Then the great secret settles on everything,
you're sleeping and I launch out into darkness;
ivy pours into the courtyard, I'm half drowned,
face emerging in Spring – Dionysus.

*

Even the island I speak from is painted by Hilton,
to the rhythm of dropped seeds into instant oleander
and open mouthed cats into swaying boughs;
the riot of ants know the plan
and blue drips from the mighty swimmer.

Interior darkness dissolves in the air
and perfect weather wraps us bodies;
hand in hand like nerve ending sex
my eyes have seen the glory
riding in on a big clam shell.

Let the breeze stir and sing,
lift the shirt off the girl with ample breasts
and cool the hairy god slumped in the breakers;
the two master is trim, we're ready to leave,
the white circuit snaps and ignites.

The all-sea shines lit from below,
children's voices scud across the bay
quick ripples enskied in acrylic;
– will you wait for me there?
on the shore of the morning world.

*

I think of the fields at night,
the compact Celtic geometry
laid over with darkness
and the black sea rising.

The Gulf of Sleep invades my room,
waves rise with each breath
drowning thought under the door,
go down you beasts, you bastards.

In the compass of the sea
I am abandoned, absolute,
but let me keep the way
of talking to my children.

The lights on the other side
shine out clear and bright,
my boat is one word sent
in the language of my painted hands.

The shape of morning rises,
white ribbons of light
unravel across the sliding waves,
momentary chart of all the sea lanes of the world.

*

If this window opens on the world of free running senses;
your filthy mind in the cart pulled by my bonny horse
– see she prances, treading the liquefied air
falling like amber on us sorry bodies,
so that our limbs are restored, magically proportioned,
and we lie and roll and walk in one another,
the anthropometric secret in our hands at last
as easy as talk floats out of the bedroom door
across the evening laid out in this land of good weather;
the game is up – and if the window doesn't etc the game is up:
we must settle for the living creatures we have about us,
and that would be the Hilton in this earthly paradise
awake in a sea of trees breathing underground,
ambidextrous, prolific and grinning.

*

Melanie I want to say in plain words
how at night when you're sleeping
and I come to bed and you fold into me,
my hands resting on your breasts
drift into the lovely south of your belly.

I see in the dark, my hands painted your colour,
and it's too late or early and I'm awake
with work sliding down the chute
and there's no sound abroad, nothing;
only my mind full of you sleeping.

My love, stir and fold into me again,
turn over to me your naked self;
let me taste your swimming body,
catch you again in the great waterfall.
How on earth did I find you?

Out on the circuits of stupid chance,
along the burnt-out motorways of nowhere,
in public buildings dressed in a suit;
there you're saying – What did you dream about?
My mouth hanging open in a new world.

*

Yellow slabs of light rest between the houses
and the names of streets are lost this morning;
earth colours flatten out, it could be winter.
I'm in the pathless dark with the spooks
doing the low drift over the smoky roofs.

The whole thing shrinks to a few acrylic strokes,
congealed and pulsing momentary scribble
to make the world again,
what was barren adorned
what was fallow the green riot.

The cat saunters along the tower wall,
over the birdless branches
she carries the piled up sky on her back,
through a blue gap time is sliding away
and the Hilton sea shouts Roll Up Roll Up.

⋆

All night the sea broadcasts white rage,
the radio plays dumb, drowned in the pelting air,
and I launch the box on the bobbing waves
– inside my wife, my children, my home.

My hope is all enclosed in that thought,
there's nothing to be done in tearing space;
foxes and magpies on the roof sharpen their knives,
there's nothing personal about it, just their nature.

It's the ancient world calling, are you receiving me?
High in the wind an aria is sounding,
my mouth is empty, my hands are claws;
come back come back, my heart answers like a beacon.

It's the ancient world calling – over.
Her hair streams back like rain,
flying fish and plastic bottles dance in strings of light
and marble giants rise from their alluvial bed.

*

The sky over the mountains in layers
steps down to the surrounding sea;
black lines drawn over the surface
rope it in, let it go, abstract picture facing.

My eyes are open forever on this,
I see the boats coming and going,
time in their wake pours in and out
and the light tilts westward.

I keep watch on the waking world,
the morning call to air sounds
and the short wave towers turn,
centre the static band of knowing.

Each grove, each bank and field
erects a column of bird song,
lifting a thousand notes into the air
rising and falling in apparent chaos.

The birds singing make the sun rise
and figures released emerge again;
the woman walking to the first house,
limbs proved in earth, kinetic.

Sing birds sing, tune up the day,
blow the wild flowers electric leaping
along the roads of Spring's republic
where she sets her foot this way.

*

Stick it in your pipe, said the Hilton
and the moment is expansive and English;
a potential life, a deep breath taken
rising from the 1950s, a fresh wind over the fields;
let me walk you around the animal town.

We are winning, so stick it in your pipe;
smell the sea in the air, we could live like this
unaccounted for in serious clothes,
the light in waves making the hidden form apparent
shapes the dark door in the burning wall.

So we escaped to Antibes, a new world,
and the work flowed in beats;
we ate the good bread in the white mornings,
saw the days sail by like painted boats
at a jaunty angle in a square of painted blue.

Each day was a gem in the anatomy of the sea,
each facet of the red flowers, the free woman,
the dog, the horse and the black scribble of my love;
and on that ripe, round occasion
Captain Bottle saw the truth and jumped ship.

And with my right hand and my left hand
I made the picture of it all.

Alexiares

My Journey to Euripides

Because I knew my Euripides I survived the Latomiae,
I was of the 4,000 of the quarries;
we saw the ships go down, the sea burning
and the passes of the fertile plain blocked.

Those who did not die were sold as slaves
– somewhere to the south? I don't know;
others, like me, a few, climbed out on poetry,
the Syracusans like poetry.

But they did not see, on my inner arm,
the tattooed ivy, immortal imprint
of the immigrant stranger, lord of many names,
they did not see I was of the god of all blossoming things.

In the pit I remembered the spring when I was a boy;
in my village we observed the rites,
the year I was chosen, both parents alive,
the procession of all of us made the round.

> We walked with the year, the season
> of trees alive and the rocks moving,
> rumours took on flesh in the mountains
> and at night on the water light sang.
>
> I remember Hermes gave me moly
> that I might resist her,
> white flower, black root
> that I might have her.
>
> We ran to the high meadows
> out of the arms of the leaping god,

        the wet earth his chamber
        spring tripping in our wake.

After I had recited my way out of the pit,
I went aboard a merchant ship across the Ionian;
I swam with the low life of small fishes and other fauna,
driven by brigandage and buggery mostly.

You can spend days staring at the surface of the sea,
the gulls wingtip acrobatics, feed me feed me,
the occasional blue fin and the confused bee
– staring in fact at the glossy reflection of nothing.

It has meaning in a lost language of sound
sliding across the water and familiar harbours;
smoke drifted over the ruined villages
and starving fishermen threw dog shit at us.

By slow stages and different ships I went south;
all along the Peloponnese the same story,
a war economy with the wheels coming off
and rumours of the big crisis to end the world.

A storm wrecked us into the Messenian Gulf,
we came into the first harbour still open;
Helen's brothers stood on the rock called Pephnos
and on the water I heard the songs for Leukothia.

The village was empty of people
and I knew they would be out in the fields
at the ceremony of return and uprising,
the greater journey of the earth.

We cooked the pots of all the seeds,
the white poppy, barley, pulse and lentils
but not for human food
nor for the strengthless heads of the dead.

But for the earth people, to take down with them
for the unimagined harvest,
carried to all our weddings
when the fields rise up and each root blossoms.

We don't eat abstractions,
we burn pigs, snakes and fir cones
in a blackened hole to make the earth part,
for the unimagined harvest.

I went south in the oven of summer
around the bare finger of land for Matepan,
those days the sea filled my mind
and Laconia filled my mouth.

The submarine cave into hell was crowded,
victims of a precept blown half way across the world;
poor souls – no ghost of mallow, asphodel or orchid
flowered in the burnt dust under their feet.

And further east I arrived at Trozen
to hear the white women singing all night,
love wanders in the high meadows
in every atom of the swollen sea.

I kept Euripides before me and made for Attica;
they said Athena was lost,

all argument over and the squares empty;
incarnate city of the mind left to slow rot and irrelevance.

I remembered Pericles's speeches,
their perfect syntax cut from marble
singing over our heads in the market place,
we repeat them even as we fall.

Those monuments of the air,
made from what is sweet and what is terrible,
drove us on to meet what came
– by then I'd had my fill of both.

Later, when Spartans planned to raze the lot,
with Euripides silent in final exile,
one voice rose to sing his words
and no hand was lifted against Athena.

Well, my soul was pastured there too;
unscorched by invasion, in the glories of knowledge,
my journey became a perfect map of itself
and I walked in two worlds with each step.

I had been north through the Vale of Tempi,
mountains piled up, wall upon wall of snow
polished by the sun, serrating the world,
the passes gone over to a sort of blindness.

Did everything turn to a whiteness in the end?
Even the turquoise sea in a white rage
lifted each wave into a booming nothing
and the levelled plain was not the floor of heaven.

I found him at the court in Macedon,
I was not the first to make the journey;
in the bowl of the mountains, at the end of reason
the great mind near empty.

He looked like bones collapsed, half blind,
fit for the dogs or whatever ceremony was there;
his breath like a bird passing
made one note in the frozen sky.

I am Alexiares of the Latomiae,
I stood where Athens over reached itself
and landed in a hole, 4,000 at my shoulder;
I stand opposed, above ground in the air.

I repeated each word, each strophe
lifting me out of the pit,
out of the dumb quarry into the light;
and the seas and islands echoed him.

> I am Dionysus, lord of many names,
> of the bull, the snake, the lion
> mixing all forms of life;
> I glide over the pit.
>
> The city is drowned in ivy,
> I will give you what you want
> and the streets and precincts catch light.
> Is it dawn rising, my fresh girl?
>
> I am Dionysus, I call in my own
> from the fields of Lydia and Phrygia;

when the cup is empty, even to the shadow,
I am manifest, the empire of confidence.

Odes of Alexiares

1
The thing is Imperator, you don't rage in the Capitol
nor in the tents of the enemy but sip nectar with empurpled lips,
and your ministers dance around a mound of dirt
moulded in the likeness of Leo Strauss.

So thought stalks Babylon along unmade roads
and ignites a village of unknown women;
you can smell it seep into the circuit of mineral rivalry,
you can see it inflate a mighty god of swords.

The style of the project here is cinder block houses,
and with the order sent we have to finish the job;
misinterpretation razes another town on the bloody edge,
it flickers then evaporates in the western syntax.

The thing is Imperator, you open your mouth of lethal zero
and in another country the sky is sucked down a roaring tunnel.

2
'Accept our offer of a carpet of gold or we bury you
under a carpet of bombs.' And before the snows fall etc.

Negotiation whispers down the pipeline, Pax Americana,
pronounced regime change one bright morning.

Pronounced the Caspian region is the key,
the Bridas bid ended with the assassination of Masood.

Before the snows fall etc, one bright September morning etc.

3
I know that my speaking to you is as pointless as raising my hand to a hurricane; listening as if to speak words to the circling sky of full spectrum dominance. Call things what they are; you never swung out into theory neutral space but had them read 2.5 million pages, covering the trail to that day.

On that morning was the fire a thousand degrees short of what it takes to burn a steel framed building? Was the steel sold off to China and Korea as scrap before forensics got a look in? How quiet are the answers? As quiet as a flight for Saudis in a total flight ban? And the captain went a singing through the fields of bright flame, 'Go massive. Sweep it all up. Things related and not.'

4
I would have you study these Hazara war rugs,
though they are not easy to read the images speak,
hand made and stained with vegetable dyes.
The Taliban murdered the Hazara, village by village,
late converts to Islam, with good faces from the Mongols.

Can carpet design convey irony?
The bold colours and childlike shapes
of B52s, stinger missiles and tanks
in the style of first generation video games,
would make the rug fit a boy's bedroom.

Stick men jump from the towers,
first and second impact are marked;
the noses of the aeroplanes disintegrate
and at the foot of the scene
an aircraft carrier floats off, as if distracted.

Across the middle of the towers
a dove flies uniting the flags
of America and Afghanistan;
most of the words remain unreadable
– THE TEARURS WAR IN THE AMEIRCAN

Here, Imperator, you can see,
the sky sucked down a roaring tower
and the words remain unreadable;
the border of abstract flowers is carefully executed,
soft cream and sage green on a band of dull red.

Interview

Q. How did you get here?

At night from 36,000 feet fire
rages in the bowl of the mountains
a thunderstorm caught lightning
ignited again and again my god
I've heard the pine trees explode
on the smoking hills and cowered.

Q. What are you doing here?

When Roza Eskenazi sings
I fall under that wave.
How's it going Roza my child?
Aman, I sing and spit and swoon.
She will strip your heart
cleaner than the sea.

Q. Do you want to leave?

Leave this screen of Tamarind and Eucalyptus
surrounding our aerial garden?
The limby green layer of living things
breathes on us painted out ghosts,
by morning the white frame made empty
and the day pauses in mountain air around us.

Alexiares in Exile

1

After the last journey I began another,
though not exactly Ithaka, despite Cavafy;
I opened my instructions in a different country,
sailing blind in the sea lanes of Morse code.

The sun strikes the tower, a massive gnomon;
time is nothing here, over and out
the land running south in blue layers,
the villagers call it a promontory of song.

It rises as a sort of Egypt of now and then,
a land bridge of animals and plants
for Martin Bernal to dance across
so that imports follow in strict measure.

An early naturalism, alive and immediate,
the African Blue Lily or Agapanthus,
your name in a burning circle on the ground:
work it out by next dispatch.

2

Again last night the sun died red into the sea,
this is hardly news I know but the sky caps the black
and my mind is elsewhere over the singing water;
engine of the world, ace of ambition, floored me.

Thalassa Mavri they sing, well they might – Greeks;
I am in exile between textual variants,

head down in darkness dancing out such poems
would make the emperor of goats weep.

Here I barely stick to the rim of the world,
a brown river and a thin wall against the hoards,
they come screaming off the frigid steppes;
it is a strange form of exegesis I suffer.

On the sea's bend sinister stands the bridgehead,
I hide behind the wall, holding a stick, shaking;
Athena – come, love me again, give me one more chance,
not this brightness pissed into a marsh under a black sky.

3

What am I doing here? How do I know?
I was sent out into this condition
with no secret gate east or west,
this is Tomis, Samos, London transit camp.

My body's made invisible to me,
a shape inside a shape of nothingness;
I float on my neighbour's language,
it leaves me undisturbed, untroubled.

They seem well disposed and incomprehensible;
the other morning they were up early,
before the sea had taken its colour
and went off singing in the woods.

Later, bread appeared on my window ledge,
it was cinnamon bread, I ate if for breakfast;
I am not speaking truth to power,
I watch the sparrows peck about the broken wall.

4

At night the sea piles up its sound,
no one will sail against this wall of water
and the mind falters, sliding off the wind
over the boats abandoned in the harbour.

Smoke thickens and songs by Xylouris go round,
– at one time all these songs were banned;
the little red tanks of the eager insurgents
arrive in waves, their eyes like heavenly spheres.

Will we survive the brilliant strategy?
security calculated in ships which sink;
they say the logos was constant in Athens,
all aliens thick-tongued barbarians: what nerve.

I held the idea of an island suspended
in the deep sea between three continents;
and this song can make you drunk,
just listen and you will be big time intoxicated.

5

When I walk through the streets of mud,
between the wooden palisades and nephos,
garish billboards cover the sky
sending the dumb dumb message mainstream.

I walk out of their dream, the war on abstract nouns,
and see we have fallen into the hands of thieves,
the barbarians who need barbarians
to make the bloody business spin.

After the blast I witnessed illumination;
the family photographs tattered but untouched,
poor souls they flew away at last
but nothing will replace the absence of your face.

A massive darkness sits on my shoulder,
I float in the broken signal of the short-wave;
all night the black sea spits out our first language
and the streets falter in earthy tracts.

6

I found co-ordinates to prehistoric creatures
lying frozen in rock pools, the first cuneiform;
a music like letters in polished scales
lifting up from the earth every spring.

I found the uncovered mosaic on the cape,
a ditch, a temple, a chapel and god

the model worked – but if the ground gives way
no bloody aroko of the Rebus tribe will save you.

Nor does the meaning of the sky vary
– trail of stars, boom: trail of stars, stop:
those who sent me don't see the indifference,
how perfect syntax dismantled Ilium.

And god the beautiful trees of the mountain
in banks and hills go rising up,
like promised countries around the world
the beautiful trees opened their arms.

7

Rain has released the smell of wild garlic
and splashed blue cyclamen across the path;
mosaic of light on the insect-laden air
bears the unfinished music of the small gods passing.

In darkness the outboard of the fishing boat
binds the edge of a black sea blanket
and marine white noise floods the frontiers of the world,
the work songs of the faithful at the final catch.

In these lost villages of the terraced mountains
the most complex ladders to the stars
were made by Ottoman musicians,
masters of the clarino, the sisters of amanes.

And all night I hear them shape from the air
the heavenly body of our starry queen,
they open a door in the endless sky
with Apollo's bees dancing attendance.

8

The sun strikes the tower, a massive gnomon,
time is nothing here, over and out;
on the collapsed ramparts of the golden west
they have lost the power of naming.

What am I doing here? I don't know.
My neighbours sing – the black wall of the far one
leans over us closely tonight – I would not surrender
one moment of happiness to explain this to you.

It looks like Apollo, the whole singing world,
laid out across the grey slab,
but there's no end of feeling in the sky
and the lights of home are like poured honey.

The wind is looking to blow the village flat
and the sea boils in a white rage at the harbour wall,
a child in a wedding dress over her jeans and trainers
flits from door to door like a bird.

From Alexiares's Separate Notebooks

Three village children walked into the courtyard last night,
they stood in a line singing and ringing triangles
– may St. Basil bless you, a long life on your house;
this was for new year's eve and a reward of sweets.

The boy Apollo, both parents alive, would lead the children
in our procession of the spring, they would strike the door and sing
– all time is blossoming, green stick, dry stick, young shoot sprout,
strike the door and anyone in the path of the risen year.

I heard triangles ringing across the whole country,
an Orthodox suite for a thousand manic bell towers;
may there be a long life for your house the air chimes,
teach us your alphabet St. Basil, the voices rising call.

*

At night on the corner of the post office
Hermes of the underworld takes flight,
his jet steam curls and sense of purpose
alights on the thin faced Albanian boys.

The 15 Euros a day labourers smoke and commune,
they ride in the back of early morning pick-ups
straight backed carrying a remittance economy,
experts at shaping stone for traditional houses.

Vagelis told us, in Albania, once ago it was ok,
I had a home by the sea, a big house;
the rich countries suck in the poor across the world,
15 Euros would be for something skilled, like tiling.

The boys saunter in this easy darkness
and the village kids play slow mo football,
a balloon floating over the collective heads;
the whole scene swims in sweet air like honey.

*

Fat leaved ivy pours over the broken wall
down the sides of the Taygetos
splitting the rocks of the terraces.

I stuck my head inside the box of spring,
sweet song of flowers, frogs and birds
rising up from the green in one breath.

The day comes calling out of the blue,
on the salt pans and rock pools
the sea drops a whole synod of little gods.

*

What did Ovid do all day,
smell the harbour, count his syllables,
see the black sea light soak the wall
mapping the edge of utter darkness
and curse the frost on the face of Augustus?

I pile the white stones in the corners
for their click, the beautiful painted bodies
of the men and women who take their shapes
from the shapes of the olive groves, smoke rising
over the blue hills of the earth turning.

I follow Europa and her bull in the wet meadow,
they vanished in the spray zone's magnetic air
beaded with every singing world;
she holds on, mouth open, I don't know,
his smile lights up another country.

*

I've not written a word to you for weeks;
the Spring weather is gentle, the air like balm
has made my mind candid and I can't bear to be inside.

So I sleep and eat and fuck like a little god,
the sea shush shushing us land children
out along the shore running to the end of the world.

The village wakes to dog-barking dawn and
all the birds practise their scales in Greek,
I can feel the earth tilting into first light.

I dreamt the music of how the night comes
in the lemon groves and orange groves of the Argolid
and walked the rising hills to the village of lights

Towards a mask of gold, behind which there's no darkness,
only the dreaming air sweet as mountain honey;
here it comes, here comes the night, the Beautiful Door opening.

*

I have not told you enough about last night in the Albanian taverna
where the wine is deep and takes you down with it;

these boys in their red nylon jumpers and football shirts
– Sweden 1986, the poorest of the poor of Europe, Jesus
their ring tones and house building for English and Germans;
in this absurd channel of the world market a Chinese girl
walking from village to village, now goes table to table
not selling plastic toys and watches to displaced peasants;
you almost imagine a country they've left at home.

They are gentle in their manners under the American film,
under the presence of men like Alec Baldwin actors;
heavy on the common air the atomized cash circulates
around the table where Ovid stares, writing letters Roma / Amor,
save me Augustus from these fucking barbarians;
– next time you come and dance in Albania;
the big screen blonde in a blonde bikini in blonde America
snaps the boy's eyes like magnets to attention,
then they return to their beer and smoke and courtesies.

Ritsos tips his head to the glide and wail of the clarino,
his hands hold that face in the mountain village,
rearranging the white stones of his risen nation;
an archipelago of men and women reach across the Aegean.
Look Ritsos, off in the corner, the wrecked sailor stands,
Ithaka the birthmark in the crook of his left arm;
he wants to write the final chapter, straight as an arrow;
and then we can scatter the bloody pages of the kanun
in the mouth of the harbour to feed the silver fishes.

– And next time you dance the deep wine in Albania,
the clarino rising over any mountains and valles we have to hand,
its slide and figuration describes what land this is Illyria lady
and I am letting the little iambs out into the fields;

we do a kaba, berati say, and then step it up koftos for a wedding,
– I thought it was from Epirus, yes yes is all the same music;
I am letting the little riot, wave the flaming napkin, then step
over the border, see, the generations in my feet, step
the frontiers disappearing dance, and step step.

⋆

Beyond all of this with morning just risen
a rumour in the mountain villages,
the white horse runs from his shadow.

Nostrils sharp as fluted marble,
the vaporous sun streams from his flanks,
muscles flicker in one wave.

Pulse beating on the chambered earth,
the white horse in the high meadow
runs over terraces of light.

Ulysses in the Car

Melanie, I'm in the dark car staring, where are you?
and the keys? The sky unlocked pours lament
along the cold slot where I wait at the foaming gutter;
enough of this place, the great divide is real.

The house is full of darkness, the wine we poured
unfit for breathing or the brimming crowd;
my mother transparent before me could not stand
without my help, now rises in that company.

Melanie where are you? Are you driving home
between the low warehouses and shamefaced politics
plotted across our country? Are you cutting a smart V?

I see your face suspended in the great, dark rush,
faint interior lights daisy below your gaze, ignite
the bright metallic splash as you open the door.

From the Holiday Inn Athens
by the blue neon bridge
the ancient sites have been tested
with earthquake simulation.

The temple of Zeus withstood 6.5,
its size and design triumphant;
the theatre of Dionysus unmoved
as if speaking truth to power.

At night the city is a bowl of light
offered up by the Penticlean Hills,
from the dark altar of the orchestra
the world will hear you whisper.

*

Pinter in a wheelchair
performs *Krapp's Last Tape*
not even on his last legs,
it is beyond drama.

The act will stand unlike
the adventures of Wolfowitz and Rumsfeld,
the fantasies of Leo Strauss
burning in the desert.

Aeschylus wrote *The Persians*
from the viewpoint of a defeated enemy
after fighting the battle of Marathon:
imagination alive imagine.

*

Daunted by the five hour drive
we paused at the door of the day,
then with morning sped to the west
across Attica, the Argolid and Arcadia.

From the Holiday Inn Athens
we know the way forward,
by the villages that defeated Sparta
and the road-side shrines of lives saved.

The sky opens over the secret valleys,
the tractor towns and their satellites;
on the other side of the blue dome
a girl's voice, high and driven, sings.

Each green field my god the waves of grass
flooding over the hills break your heart
to the first of the houses we're all awash
and you came in like the genius of the rolling tide.

The telephone wires radiate from the pole
holding the sky aloft a thousand messages of
are you there can I speak the weather here is
the accident of us falling together into.

The conspiracy of your shape, your colour
touch me the substance of you I want to
have eat and fuck in that gold jacket
silk with the little clear buttons like rain.

There's a name for the work on the big loom
you tell me as you walk on this side in the shining air.

Outside rain rains in this room
with only Pritchard for company,
vegetation luxuriates from the earth
[approximately 37 lines destroyed]

The poem speaks of endless war.

I seized the Lebanon entire
and cleaned my weapons in the deep sea;
you liberators will not have sweets and flowers,
there will be none: my name is mighty.

The people I sing to are dead.

You will hear my music in Mesopotamia,
beards and banjos, the Baptist sentiment
for fools to mouth in the public square,
see the river gods turning their backs.

I cut down stonepine, cypress, many nations,
the air thick with fragrant dust
settles on my men like a blessing,
like tributes of gold, boxwood and rich garments.

The Pax Augusta does not stand here
between the great green and the towns of mud,
Rome is far off, even the idea remote,
zealots gone west wiring faith.

For you caught on the border
the local palette will run to blood,
the markets fluctuate like genocide:
the people I am singing to are dead.

Lyric voices crowd the sea to sing his mind away,
from the secret meadow and heap of poet's bones
you see a life continue day by day on that green shore,
as if in the tradition of the music of the drowned.

What reason did for Spicer is locked in a box and sunk,
subject to 28 lbs psi, full fathom five approximately;
Coleridge is down there too, the surge in his veins
recalls the contours of the earthquake zone around Cythera.

How soft was the air when you wrote the music of the drowned?
Is that you girl leaping from the edge of the world
into a massively blue and absolute idiom,
hair spread like a dark net to catch the little poets?

Each point in the trajectory confounds impact,
the intervals are harmonised to make us leave.

The Artemision Tunnel is Two Kilometres Long

Between the Mountains of Artemis and Lyrkio
crossing from the Argolid to Arcadia – switch on your lights –
we drive into the black tunnel, the eye of day closed.

Artemis, lady of all the animals and living things,
lead us into darkness, lead us under the mountain of your shrine.
Can we even breathe down here? We are in your hands.

If the earth drips off roots threaded through our eyes,
lady of the wild things, light-carrying Artemis,
our theme is order and the springs of Inachos rise with you.

On higher ground, surrounded by the hall of trees,
the sacrifice is without distinction, all living things
– oxen, goats and ending with small birds, thrown into the pyre.

Flocks of quail crowd the sky, as thought flies without shadow,
red hem at the knee, date palm, stag and bee, we see all of this;
against the city of unjust men she tries her bow.

The Alphios marks the boundary where her genius attends,
and after the fire in the artificial forest
I see my own family in a bright circle restored.

My parents, my children and the familiar dead stand again
at the stations of the road, westward from her hands
we climb the high, watered meadows around Asea.

The sky is empty above this temenos of orchard and arable land;
there's a garage, a collapsed house and an abandoned speed trap,
and we stand again in the great common field.

Another day pours down light in waves
and the sea settles a blue question around us;
one end of the earth at our feet, the other falls away
beyond the aerial terraces stepping into the sky.

The English newspapers have gone from the shop
and the village retreats into itself for the season.
With no other island to find, what if our bodies fit?
suspended here, not even waiting, what black ship?

Where is the map of anxieties, the darkness chartered?
Apart from all that grows, nothing rises and falls;
the idea that the idea that – O Xenophanes, genius poet,
what have we done since you spoke?

There's no proposition written on the wide air
but the waves breathing whiteness into the world.

When the Spartans came over the mountain
and made us their slaves,
self-appointed lords of the way it is
with their global credit, pipelines
and smart weapons in phalanx,
our irrelevance came to an end.

The hills at a certain hour turned mauve
and these men emerged in our fields
as if out of nowhere, clouds around their thighs,
their mouths barking – Helot – Barbarian – Outdweller;
they made Leuctra into an arms dump
and the crypteia proved themselves at night.

We had invented six languages in the dust,
mastered the olive, grape and grain
and tied the knots in an epic poetry;
on discs of light dropped by the gods
we walked the broken path of the sea
and still knew the songs the birds sang.

Your picture of the world can be undone,
stations off the air, iron ore shipped out;
the sky as blue, the terraces of the sea rise and fall
enough to break your heart each morning;
we no longer walked the ground,
the earth a shadow for another's empire.

Nameless on the water, nobody steps ashore,
she sees that other life unravelling on the threshold.

It could be the picture of a man returning,
if not on the loom then in the air of all her thought;
his deep red running on the blue sea stripe,
the cleverness in her hands binding their bodies together.

Birds dyed and sewn, fish of spun wool,
a bull dancing in a field of flowers,
a border of black ships turning;
to forget the liquid beauty of linen was like death.

Carded on her thigh or the fitted onos,
terracotta shell of her absence held her;
the slow television of her longing held her
and could not be unpicked for the whole world.

The investigation remains live
into the mind its own place to make,
westbound eastbound darkness into darkness
the circle line around the world.
Shall I meet you there before work?

The knights of monotheism wear
white T shirts, dark jackets and baseball caps;
they are happy, euphoric, it is the calling
I make du'a, the people I am singing to
– she is my sister, he is my brother.

The knights of monotheism, their good deeds,
riding the circle line, their good deeds;
a virtue free of forensic analysis,
the belief in mythology as fact
comes roaring out of the tunnel.

The investigation is the glamour of his lordship,
the siege of Jerusalem, his sumptuous gifts
for the continuation of the campaign,
the [army] [made an] at[tack]
from the [tem]ple I went out again[st] abomination.

Britons and non-Britons, Christians, Muslims,
those of other religions and none,
– Shall I wait for you before work?
comes roaring out of the tunnel,
the investigation is the singing of the dead.

If we walk by Christeas's tower above the harbour
to the Greek and Latin sea at the centre of the world,
swim in the bowl of waters cool and deep,
not even the dead will call over the white signals.

There's another life radiant on the dark tide
and we're released into it, limb by limb.

I was awake thinking of two bodies asleep,
side by side in that unvisited country;
I set my thoughts to your breathing
and we went bobbing out into the gulf.

I think I dreamt it at the courtyard gate
and saw the painted waves supporting us,
out past the automatic lighthouse at Matepan
along the magnetic sea lanes for Ithaka.

After the final mountains we roll down to the sea
south from Kalamata around Taygetos on the Aeriopoli road,
and this is meant to be the literal poem of that journey,
one of a series joining seven songs in transit
as if your whole life comes in on the glimmering tide.

The road turns in a certain way and you see everything,
along this coast where gods and babies are washed ashore
out of the sky into the doorways of abandoned villages;
you can pull up and buy oranges, potatoes, honey
from the last ones alive in unpopulated places.

In the meadows and olive groves myth takes root,
paths in the hills lead there, if you can crawl and scramble;
the snake renews itself and polyphonous birds call,
strophe by strophe in the month of fair sailing
the world takes off to a single tone breaking underground.

The road turns in a certain way – miss it and you die;
ceremonies lift the earth people, gibbering at the edge,
and the voice from the well asks – what do you want?
The route is lined with bright and useless answers,
as if anything could keep us from the great descent.

Where the land ends Helen's brothers look out for us,
striding over the contours of the sea, they say;
as candid waves explode on harbour walls
a girl from Cythera rises, from the epicentre,
to leave us drenched and shining in shock.

Eroding even the walls of Neriton
the subterranean fresh water stream
rises in the harbour or further out;
I dreamt I swam into its frozen heart.

How strange it looks to wake up on this beach
without speaking the word for stranger;
it's because I am thinking of you in that house,
wearing the dress with the splash of red roses.

I'm thinking what it is to sleep with you,
of the delight that settles on me in your shape,
and how I taste the first language in my mouth
articulate in your hands through which I move.

Until morning light rolls out into the gulf
and the backward turning sea beats time.

Coda

If one day
you hear singing
from the street
it's the colour
the thickness
of her hair
a waterfall
a blessing
the song said
the light when
I was the king
of the ocean
my kingdom ran
around the world
you reigned there
by my side
before even
Orpheus was
sounding don't
turn away
listen before
I died the
song was

Notes

Jenkyns is a translator of Sappho.

'Alstonefield' is a long poem by Peter Riley, published in the eponymous book by Carcanet Press in 2002. Roza is Roza Eskenazi, rebetika singer in the Smryna style.

'Basil Bunting and Dylan Thomas in Tehran': see the letters of Dylan Thomas.

The epigraph 'Over the calm, clear shining water . . .' is an anonymous fragment in *Greek Lyric Poetry* by M.L. West. There are also versions of Alcman and Archilocus here. See also Pritchard 'The Ancient Near East'.

Roger Hilton's Sugar
'Night Letters', Roger Hilton, 1980
'Roger Hilton', Adrian Lewis, 2003
'The Last Days of Hilton', Adrian Lewis, 1996
'Roger Hilton', The South Bank Centre, 1993
'Roger Hilton – Drawings', Jonathan Clark Fine Art, 2001
'Oi Yoi Yoi Roger Hilton', Jonathan Clark Fine Art, 2000
'Roger Hilton: An Instrument of Truth', Tate St. Ives, 1997
'Roger Hilton', Chris Stephens, 2006
'Into Seeing New: The Art of Roger Hilton', Tate St. Ives, 2006
The questions in 'From Botallack Out' are distortions of Merleau-Ponty.

Alexiares
'My Journey to Euripides': Alexiares, the speaker, is my invention; the name means one who is opposed. See Pausanias, Thucydides, Euripides, Kerenyi on Dionysus and Jane Harrison on ritual. After defeat the Athenian soldiers were imprisoned on Sicily in the marble quarries. Reciting a few lines of poetry could win freedom.

'Odes of Alexiares': for the questions in part 3 see Griffin: *The 9/11 Commission Report: Omissions and Distortions*, 2005.

'Alexiares in Exile': Martin Bernal is the author of *Black Athena: The Afroasiatic Roots of Classical Civilisation*, 1987. See Ovid's poems of exile. Nicos Xylouris was a Cretan singer. Songs by Theodorakis were banned during the Greek colonels' dictatorship.

'From Alexiares's Separate Notebooks': for kanun, the law of blood feud, the canon of Lek, see Edith Durham's *High Albania*.

Ulysses in the Car
'From the Holiday Inn Athens': the third stanza of part 2 is Paul Merchant in 'Some Business of Affinity', the introduction to a translation of Aeschylus.

'Outside rain rains in this room' takes a line from Laurie Duggan – 'the people I sing to are dead.'

'The investigation remains live' see *Report of the Official Account of the Bombings in London on 7 July 2006*.

'Nameless on the water': an onos would be fitted to a woman's leg for purposes of carding the wool ready for the loom.

'Coda': in part this poem is derived from very badly mishearing the lyrics in Offenbach's *Orpheus in the Underworld* – When I was the King of the Boeotians, which made it sound more interesting than it turned out to be.

www.ingramcontent.com/pod-product-compliance
Lightning Source LLC
Chambersburg PA
CBHW031156160426
43193CB00008B/392